BLACK INVENTORS

BLACK INVENTORS

CREATED AND DEVELOPED
by
DR. SIDNEY WALLACE

ILLUSTRATED
by
DAVID L. JOHNSON

ISBN: 1-58820-566-5

This book is printed on acid free paper

1st Books rev. 1/18/01

Foreword

Within these pages you will witness a number of individuals who have contrived and made incredible discoveries over the years that have benefited all mankind.

Inventors invent, not only to better his or her surroundings, but they also seek recognition and financial gains for their many hours of labor. There is limited information regarding black inventors. The names of many of the early black inventors were lost, leaving no history of them or their families. However, there were a few black inventors who are well known. They patented their inventions and prospered greatly.

In order to protect your invention, you must secure a patent from the U.S. Patent Office located in Washington, D.C.. A patent is the most generally accepted legal claim you can obtain for your invention to insure that you don't lose it for someone else to claim.

In 1821, Thomas L. Jennings was the first black person known to patent an invention. He was issued a patent for a dry cleaning process. He earned lots of money from this invention and used large portions of it to support the abolitionist cause.

The law of 1793 permitted slaves and freemen alike to patent their inventions. However, in 1858 the United States Attorney General put a stop to the patenting of any inventions by slaves.

Before the law of 1793, slaves frequently lost their inventions to their masters. The masters rationale for demanding ownership of their slaves inventions was that "the master is the owner of the fruits of the labor of the slave both intellectual and manual". It was not until after the Civil War that the United States made a giant step in recognizing black inventors. The passage of the

Thirteenth and Fourteenth Amendments enabled blacks to become citizens of the United States which gave them the same rights as other free men.

By the year 1870, there were countless numbers of black inventors applications on file in the U.S. Patent Office. These inventions affected the lives of people around the world, and black inventors today continue to make important discoveries.

I hope this information will serve as an incentive for all individuals to challenge themselves, develop their talents, and sharpen their skills. Who knows who will be the next to have their names written among the greats.

BLACK INVENTORS

Table of Contents

BLACK INVENTORS

THIRD EDITION

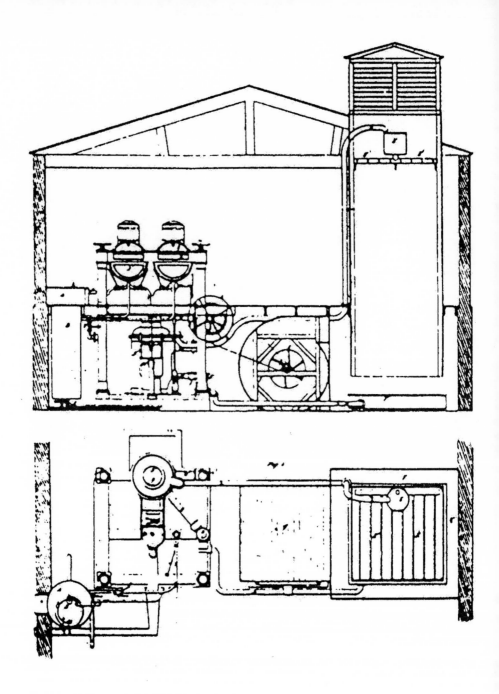

Improvement in Sugar Making

Norbert Rillieux

Invented By
Norbert Rillieux

of
New Orleans, Louisiana

Patent Date: December 10, 1846
Patent Number: 4879

Norbert Rillieux invented a new and improved way of making sugar. It was a process that involved heating, evaporating, and cooling of substances especially liquids that were used for the manufacture of sugar.

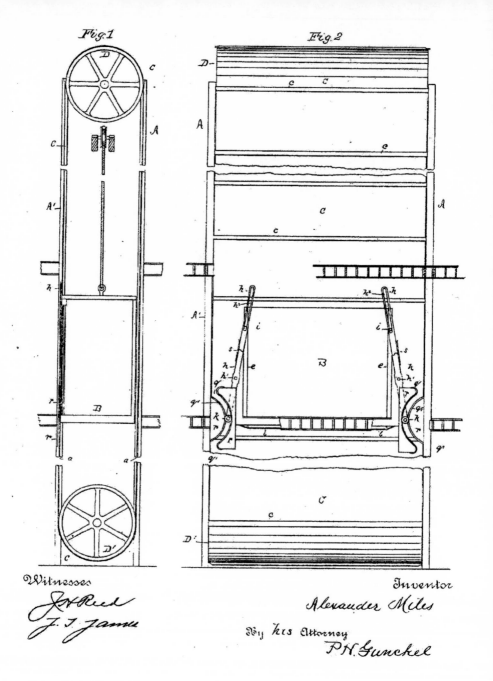

Fig.1

Fig.2

4

The Elevator

A. Miles

Invented By
A. Miles

of
Duluth, Minnesota

Patent Date: October 11, 1867
Patent Number: 371,207

    The elevator is one of the most unique forms of transportation ever invented. If it were not for the elevator, it would be almost impossible to utilize large skyscraper buildings. Transporting people and materials from one level to another within a building/structure, without an elevator would be next to impossible. The elevator has existed since the cave man in one form or the other, but Miles' invention of the closed-shaft elevator increased safety for all riders.

Fig. 1.

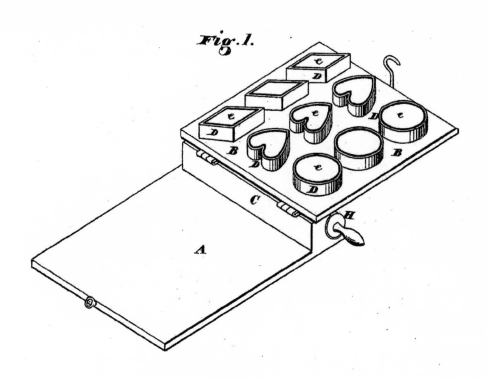

Fig. 2.

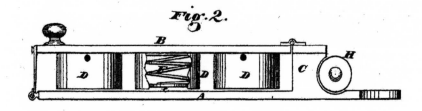

Witnesses
Geo. H. Strong.
Jno. L. Boone.

Inventor
Alexander P. Ashbonne
by Dewey
Attys

6

The Biscuit Cutter

Alexander P. Ashbourne

Invented By
Alexander P. Ashbourne

of
Oakland, California

Patent Date: November 30, 1875
Patent Number: 170,460

   The biscuit cutter is very easy to use and has not changed very much in size and shape. Ashbourne's invention improved biscuit cutting by allowing mom to cut fun shaped biscuits and lots of them at a time. All shapes and sizes of fun biscuits can be cut with Ashbourne's invention: animal cookies, Christmas cookies, the Gingerbread Man and many others.

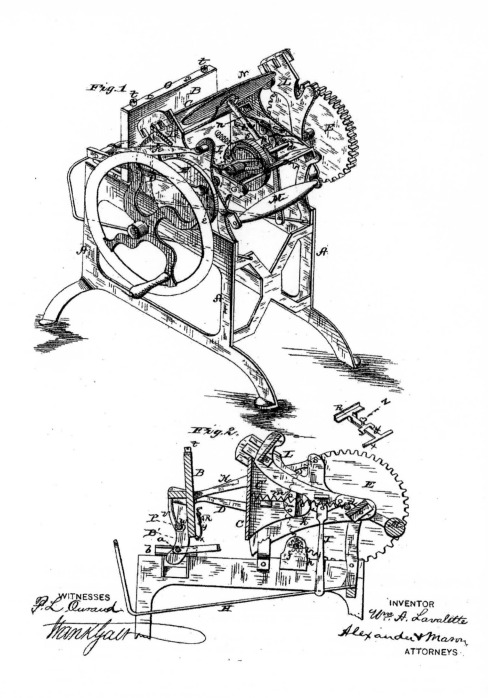

Fig. 1

Fig. 2

WITNESSES
F. L. Durand
Frank Galt

INVENTOR
Wm. A. Lavalette

Alexander & Mason
ATTORNEYS

The Printing Press

W. A. Lavalette

Invented By
W. A. Lavalette

Patent Date: September 17, 1878
Patent Number: 208,184

The printing press has made a major impact on society in terms of communication since it was introduced many years ago. Millions of people are able to read the same thing. The earlier printing presses were not very fast and the printing in many cases, was not as clear as what we have today. However, Lavalette made overall improvements to the earlier model and his improvements resulted in a printing press that is faster, user friendly, and the printing is easier to read.

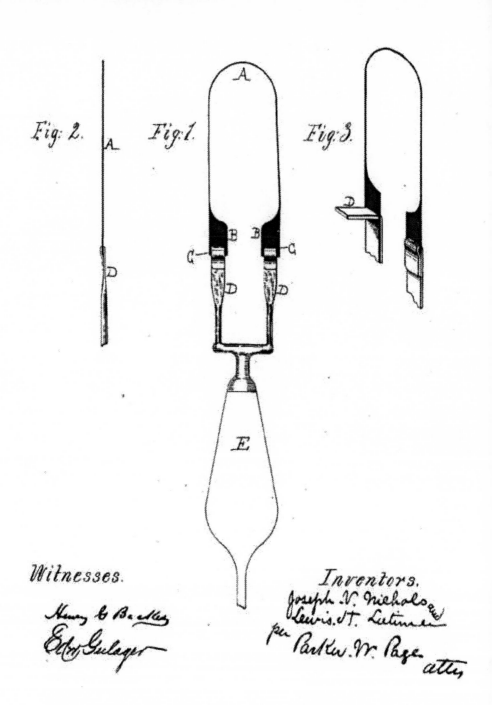

Fig: 2.

Fig: 1.

Fig: 3.

A

A

B B

C C

D D

E

D

D

Witnesses.

Henry C. Beckley

Edw. Gulager

Inventors.
Joseph V. Nicholson
Lewis H. Latimer
per Parker W. Page
atty

10

Electric Lamp

Lewis H. Latimer

Invented By
Lewis H. Latimer

of
New York City, New York

Patent Date: September 13, 1881
Patent Number: 247,097

The electric lamp was invented by two men, Lewis H. Latimer and Joseph V. Nichols, both of New York. These men invented what is known today as the light bulb. They simplified the construction of the electric lamp; by doing so they made it durable and more effective and less expensive.

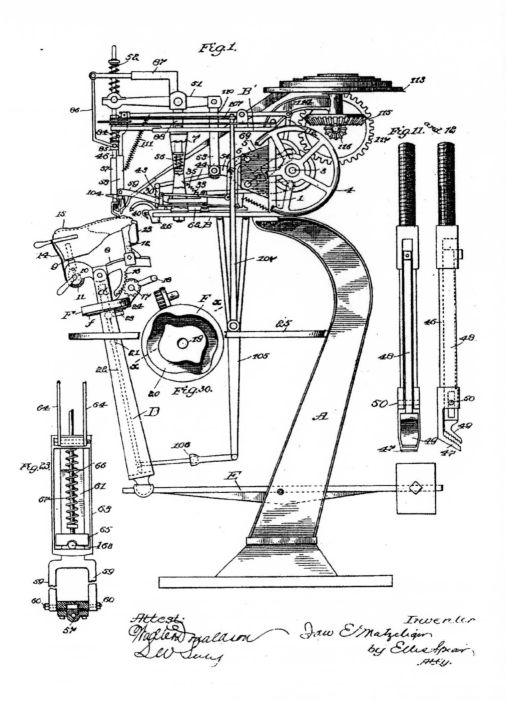

Fig. 1.

Fig. 11. and 12.

Fig. 30.

Fig. 23.

12

The Shoe Lasting Machine

Jan E. Matzeliger

Invented By
Jan E. Matzeliger

Patent Date: March 20, 1883
Patent Number: 274,207

Traveling by foot created a need for shoes. Years ago shoemakers had to sew the top of the shoe to the bottom of the shoe by hand, one at a time, which took a long time to do. This invention helped the shoe cobbler to speed the process up and make more shoes in a shorter span of time. Shoes were made better, faster and lasted longer with the shoe lasting machine.

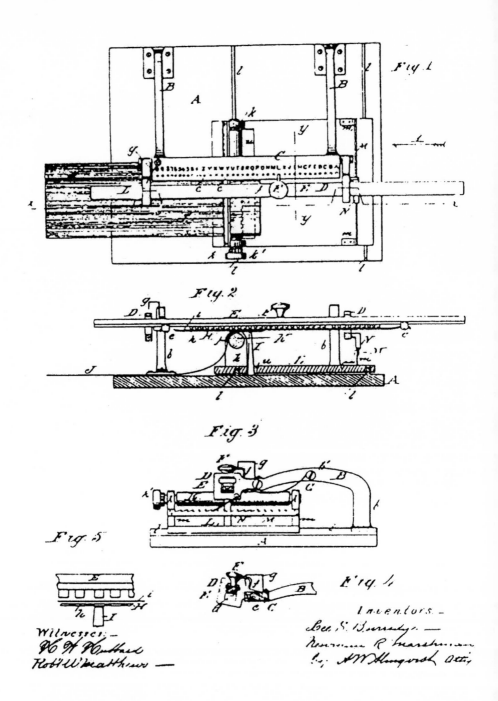

Fig. 1

Fig. 2

Fig. 3

Fig. 5

Fig. 4

Witnesses —

Inventors —

14

The Typewriter

Lee S. Burridge And Newman R. Marshan

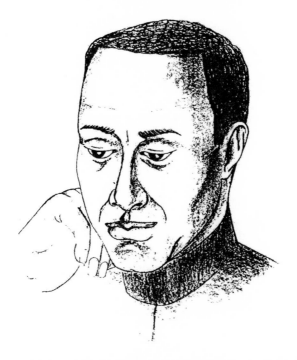

Invented By Lee S. Burridge and Newman R. Marshan
of
New York City, New York

Invention Date: April 7, 1885
Patent Number: 315,366

One of the most important office machines ever invented is the typewriter. Every individual alive today has used or will use or benefit form the use of the typewriter. They are an invaluable tool for writing.

The typewriter is the forerunner of the computer. Its basic function and operation has been instituted into today's computer.

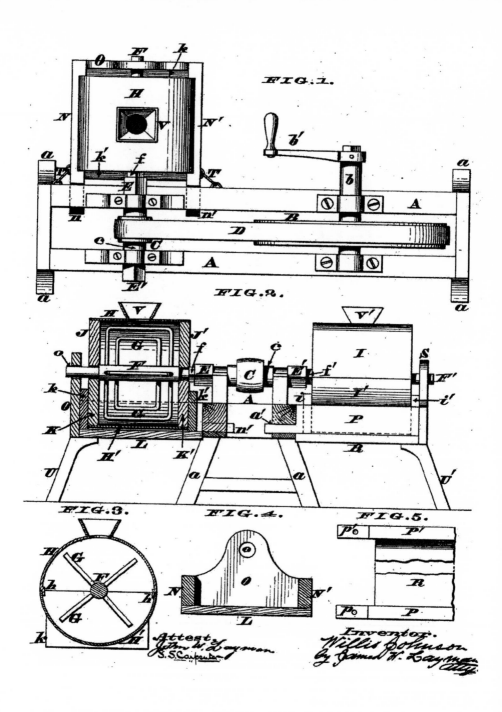

FIG. 1.

FIG. 2.

FIG. 3.   FIG. 4.   FIG. 5.

Attest
John W. Layman
S. S. Carpenter

Inventor
Willis Johnson
by James W. Layman
Atty

The Egg Beater

Willis Johnson

Invented By
Willis Johnson

of
Cincinnati, Ohio

Patent Date: February 5, 1884
Patent Number: 292,821

Scrambled eggs for breakfast is as common as breakfast itself, and in order to prepare them you must put them in a bowl, pan, etc. add whatever you wish and beat them fast, but with Willis Johnson's invention, it became easier to blend all of the ingredients together.

Willis invented a double blending machine. One that would mix on one side while the other side could be mixing something different. This way it was made possible to mix ingredients better and faster.

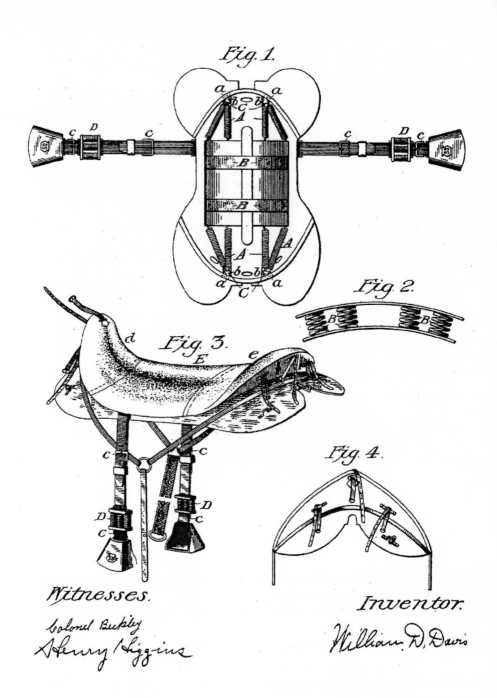

Fig. 1.

Fig. 2.

Fig. 3.

Fig. 4.

Witnesses.
Colonel Buckley
Henry Higgins

Inventor.
William D. Davis

The Riding Saddle

William D. Davis

Invented By
William D. Davis

of
Fort Assinniboine, Montana

Patent Date: October 6, 1886
Patent Number: 568,939

The riding saddle has been used in one form or another since men mounted the back of a horse, but this invention improved the saddle by making it easier to be adjusted for the rider and give strength and elasticity to the seat of the saddle. He also increased the durability of the stirrup saddle strings and straps.

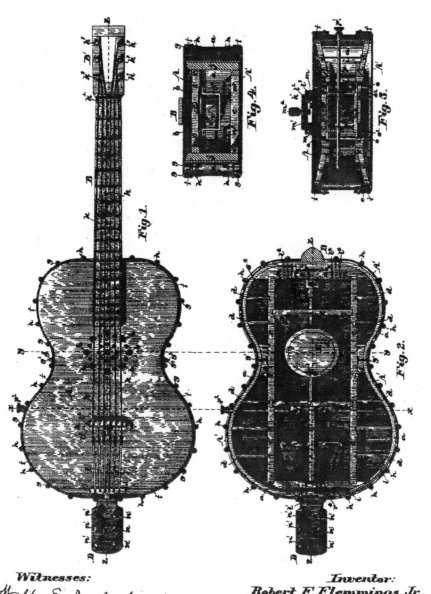

Fig. 4.

Fig. 5.

Fig. 1.

Fig. 2.

Witnesses:
Walter E Lombard
Frank E Gray.

Inventor:
Robert F. Flemmings, Jr.,
by N. C. Lombard
Attorney.

20

The Guitar

Robert F. Flemmings, Jr.

Invented By
Robert F. Flemmings, Jr.

Patent Date: March 30, 1886
Patent Number: 338,727

The guitar is a well-known instrument. There is hardly any popular music group that does not use a guitar or two as a mode of making music. It is probably the most popular instrument today.

Flemmings' improvements made it possible to experience improved melodic tones and increased volume. He also made the guitar more sensitive to the touch. This made it easier on the fingers.

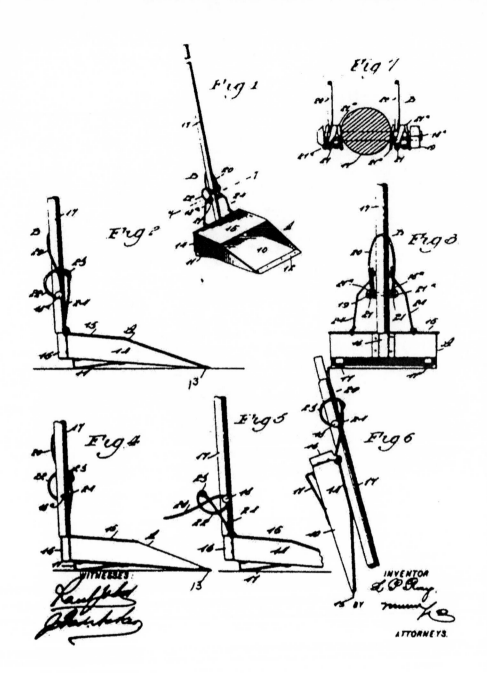

The Dust Pan

Lloyd P. Ray

Invented By
Lloyd P. Ray

of
Seattle, Washington

Patent Date: August 3, 1887
Patent Number: 587,607

The dust pan is used in almost every household in the nation and is probably one of the most well-known cleaning aids ever. It has not changed much in appearance since it was invented.

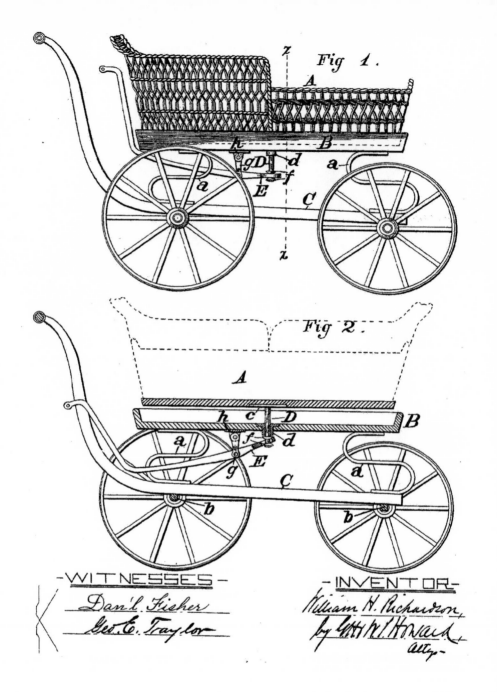

Fig 1.

Fig 2.

24

The Baby Buggy / Child Carriage

William H. Richardson

Invented By
William H. Richardson

of
Baltimore, Maryland

Patent Date: June 18, 1889
Patent Number: 405,599

The child carriage is a familiar sight for many people. It is a mode of transportation for babies and small children. Some baby carriages have hoods on top to help protect the child from the sun and rain. The first carriage was somewhat cumbersome. In order to change directions, you had to turn the carriage around.

Richardson improved the carriage by making it possible to change direction without actually turning the carriage around and disturbing the child.

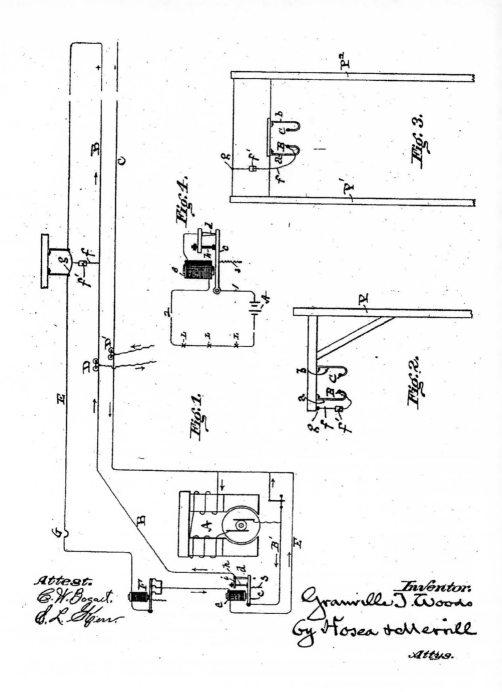

Fig. 1.

Fig. 4.

Fig. 3.

Fig. 2.

Attest.
C. W. Bogart.
S. L. ....

Inventor.
Granville T. Woods
By Hosea & Merrill
Attys.

26

The Automatic Cut-off Switch

Granville T. Woods

Invented By
Granville T. Woods

of
Cincinnati, Ohio

Patent Date: January 1, 1889
Patent Number: 395,533

The light switch as we know it today derived from this early invention by Granville T. Woods. This invention enables us to turn electric lights on and off.

Granville was the father of many inventions: the relay-instruments, telephone system and apparatus, the railway telegraph, roller coaster and steam boiler furnace, etc. He is credited with 22 inventions.

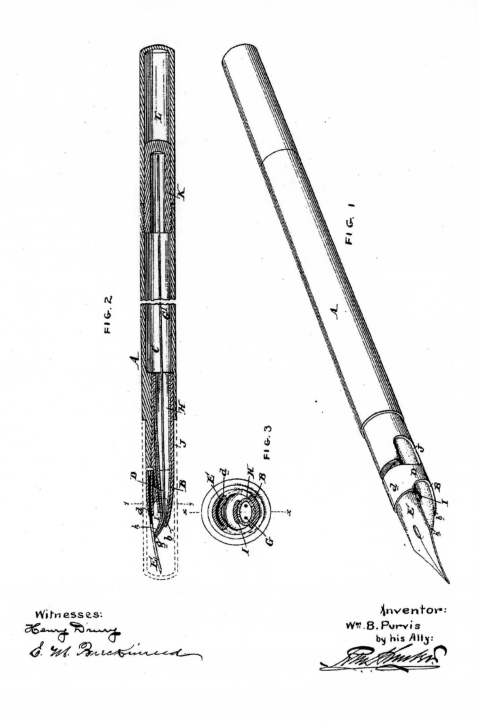

FIG. 2

FIG. 1

FIG. 3

Witnesses:

Henry Drury

E. W. Breckinreed

Inventor:
Wᵐ. B. Purvis
by his Atty:

28

The Fountain Pen

William B. Purvis

Invented By
William B. Purvis

of
Philadelphia, Pennsylvania

Patent Date: January 7, 1890
Patent Number: 419,065

The invention of the pocket fountain pen eliminated the need for carrying a separate bottle of ink. This new invention made carrying an ink writing pen a much easier task than before. It had a built-in ink reservoir that would automatically feed ink into the point of the pen.

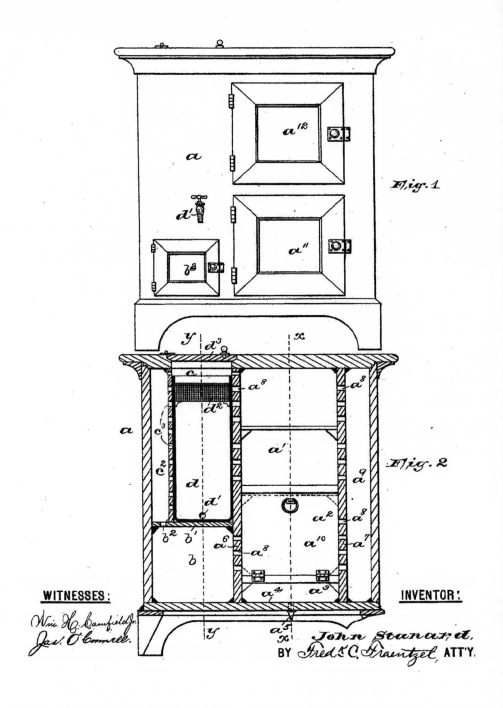

Fig.1

Fig.2

The Refrigerator

John Stanard

Invented By
John Stanard

of
Newark, New Jersey

Patent Date: July 14, 1891
Patent Number: 455,891

Years ago it was very difficult to keep food/leftovers or have a drink of cold water when you wanted it. Ice cream and cold pop/soda were a luxury, but these items soon became a daily treat for millions of people with the invention of the refrigerator. Before the refrigerator was invented, people stored their perishables in an icebox. It was based on the same principle as the cooler that keeps your soda and food cold when you go on a picnic or fishing.

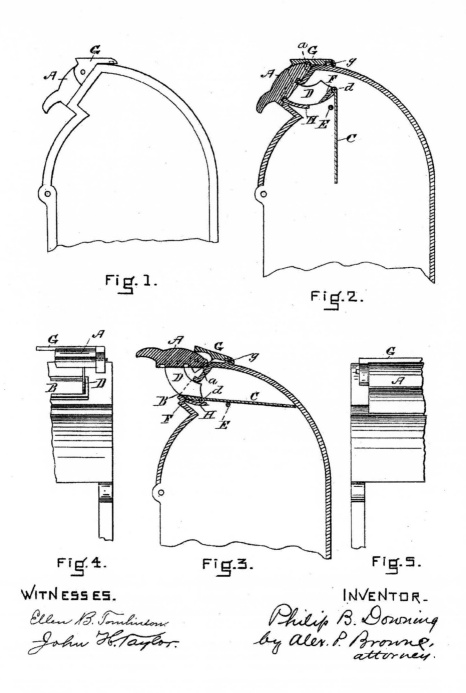

Fig. 1.

Fig. 2.

Fig. 4.

Fig. 3.

Fig. 5.

WITNESSES.

Ellen B. Tomlinson

John H. Taylor.

INVENTOR-

Philip B. Downing

by Alex. P. Browne.

attorney.

The Letter Box

Philip B. Downing

Invented By
Philip B. Downing

of
Boston, Massachusetts

Patent Date: October 27, 1891
Patent Number: 462,093

This mailbox is used by the public in almost every city and town. Downing designed this mailbox to help protect the mail, provide better accessibility and help make the mailman's job easier.

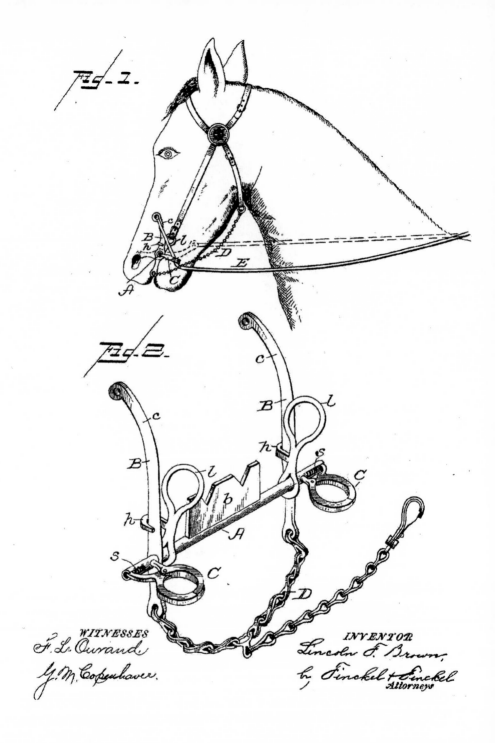

Fig. 1.

Fig. 2.

The Bridle Bit

Lincoln F. Brown

Invented By
Lincoln F. Brown

of
Xenia, Ohio

Patent Date: October 25, 1892
Patent Number: 484,994

It's not easy to stop a runaway horse. Just saying "Whoa horsey!" will not be much encouragement for a horse to stop. Lincoln Brown knew that better than anybody. He invented an improvement to the bridle bit to help control a runaway horse. The corner of a horse's mouth is very tender and the bit is place in the mouth of the horse to help him obey and is instrumental in training the horse also.

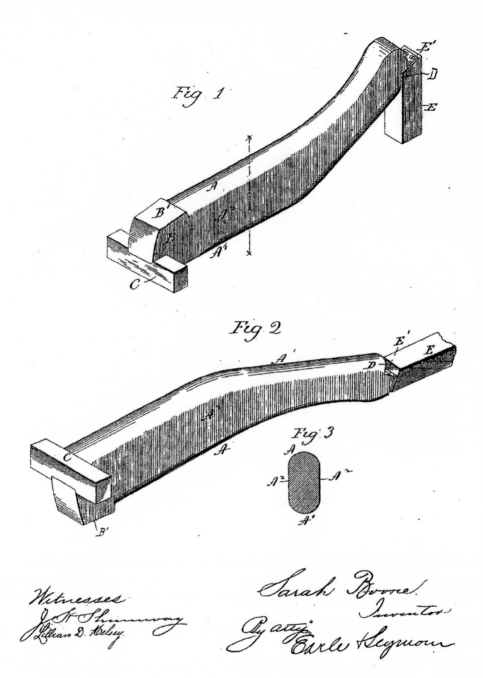

Fig 1

Fig 2

Fig 3

Witnesses
J. H. Shumway
Lillian D. Kelsey

Sarah Boone.
Inventor
By atty
Earle Seymour

Ironing Board

Sarah Boone

Invented By
Sarah Boone

of
New Haven, Connecticut

Patent Date: April 26, 1892
Patent Number: 473,653

Sarah Boone invented a very unique ironing board. This ironing board was designed to do what the regular ironing board would not do. This invention allowed you to iron the sleeves of dresses and shirts more easily and efficiently.

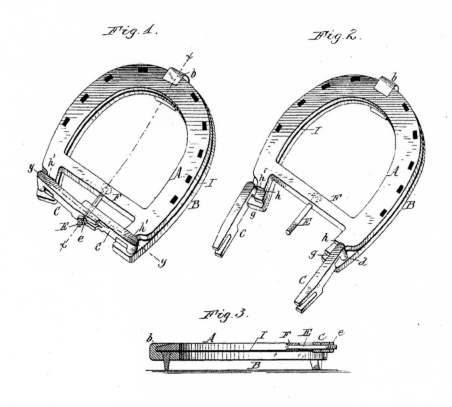

Fig.1.   Fig.2.

Fig.3.

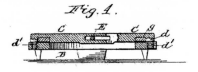

Fig.4.

Witnesses:
Emil Neukart.
Friedrich, Gustav, Wilhelm.

Oscar E. Brown Inventor.
By Wilhelm Bonner

Attorneys.

The Horseshoe

Oscar E. Brown

Invented By
Oscar E. Brown

of
Buffalo, New York

Patent Date: August 23, 1892
Patent Number: 481,271

Brown's improvements on the horseshoe made it more comfortable and easier to fit on the horse, by designing a way to cushion the horseshoe, so that it would relieve the pressure from the horse and make taking care of the horseshoe easier for the blacksmith.

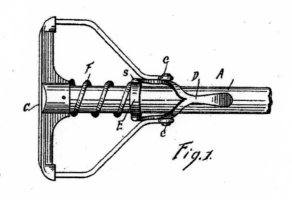

Fig. 1.

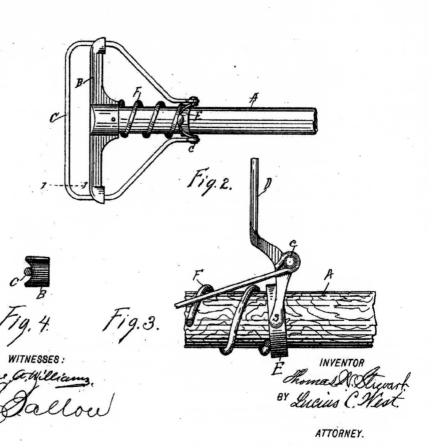

Fig. 2.

Fig. 4.

Fig. 3.

WITNESSES:
Clara A. Williams.
S. Ballou

INVENTOR
Thomas N. Stewart
BY Lucius C. West.

ATTORNEY.

The Mop

T. W. Stewart

Invented By
T. W. Stewart

Patent Date: June 13, 1893
Patent Number: 499,402

Cleaning floors is a very hard job especially if you have to scrub the floor with brushes and rags while on your knees. Well, this is just what they did years ago before Thomas Stewart invented the mop. The mop looks and serves basically the same purpose as it did when it was invented. Although there are many variations in terms of color, materials, size, etc.

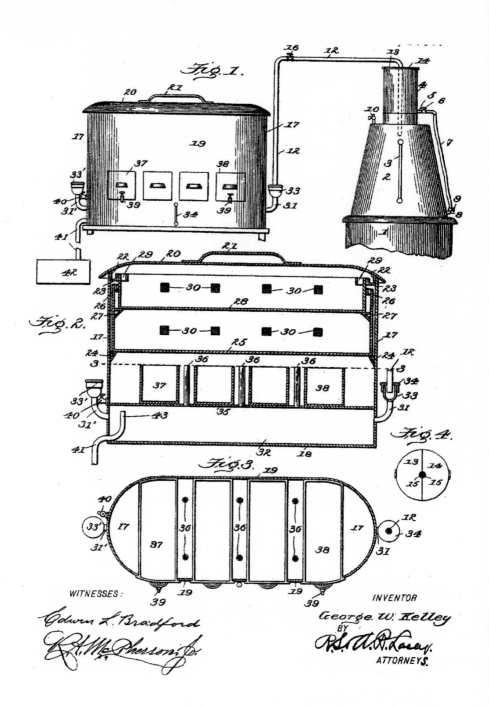

Fig. 1.

Fig. 2.

Fig. 3.

Fig. 4.

WITNESSES:
Edwin L. Bradford
R. H. McPherson, Jr.

INVENTOR
George W. Kelley
BY
R. S. & A. P. Lacey,
ATTORNEYS.

42

The Steam Table

George W. Kelley

Invented By
George W. Kelley

Patent Date: October 26, 1897
Patent Number: 592,591

Food in school cafeterias and restaurants are cooked long before they are served. Did you ever wonder how they keep food hot hours after it has been cooked. It was George Kelley's improvement on the steam table and invention of what we know today as the portable steam table, one that moves around from table top to table top. The kind you have seen in restaurants or used by a caterer.

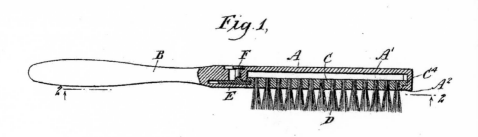

Fig. 1.

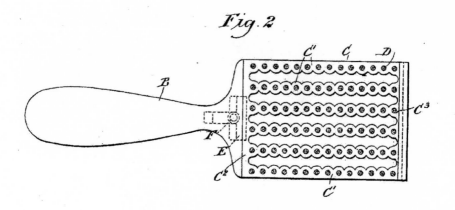

Fig. 2

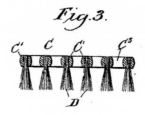

Fig. 3.

The Hair Brush

Lyda D. Newman

Invented By
Lyda D. Newman

of
New York City, New York

Patent Date: November 15, 1898
Patent Number: 614,335

The improved hair brush, as we know it today, is a well-known and recognized hair care instrument. Also, I would venture to say almost everyone has used it at one time or the other and many individuals use it daily. The brush detangles the hair, adds shine and helps with manageability.

Lyda Newman's improvement to the hair brush made cleaning the brush much easier. The brush she invented can be taken apart and cleaned.

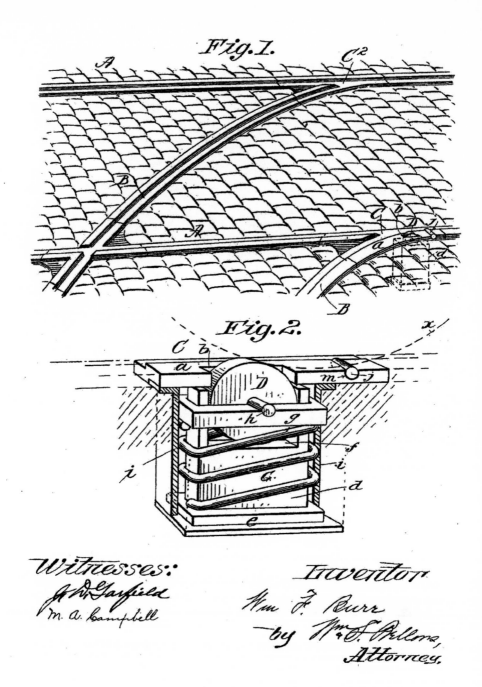

Fig.1.

Fig.2.

The Railways Switching Device

William F. Burr

Invented By
William F. Burr

of
Agawam, Massachusetts

Patent Date: October 31, 1899
Patent Number: 636,197

Long before buses and airplanes, the fastest means of travel was the train. There were tracks everywhere. Burr's invention of the switching device helped the train switch easily from one track to another while in motion.

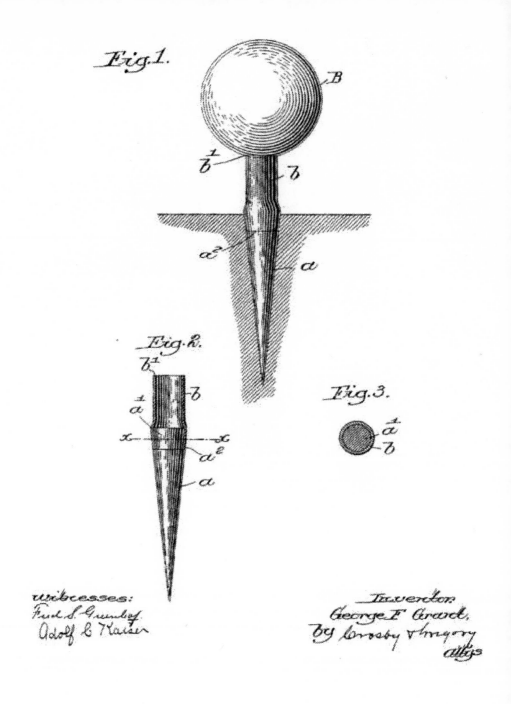

Fig.1.

B

b^1　　*b*

a^2

a

Fig.2.

b^1

a^1　　*b*

x ———— *x*

a^2

a

Fig.3.

a^1
b

Inventor:
George F. Grant,
By Crosby & Gregory
attys

Golf Tee

George F. Grant

Invented By
George F. Grant

of
Boston, Massachusetts

Patent Date: December 12, 1899
Patent Number: 638,920

This is an instrument used to support the golf ball. This invention made it easier for the golfer to hit the ball and not destroy the grass.

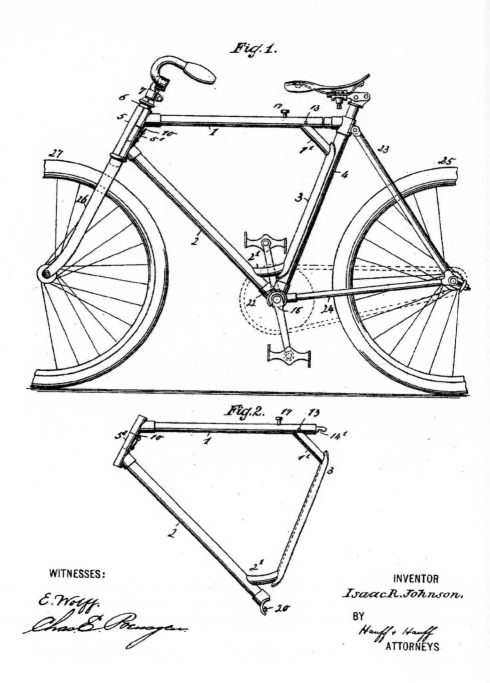

Fig. 1.

Fig. 2.

INVENTOR
Isaac R. Johnson.

BY
Hauff & Hauff
ATTORNEYS

The Bicycle Frame

Isaac R. Johnson

Invented By
Isaac R. Johnson

of
New York City, New York

Patent Date: October 10, 1899
Patent Number: 634,823

I am sure almost everyone at one time or other has been on a bicycle, either riding or riding with someone. They are lots of fun, but storage can be a problem in many cities where you use elevators, stairs, etc. In solving this problem, Johnson invented a collapsible bicycle frame; one that could be easily dismountable so it could conveniently be stored and easily carried.

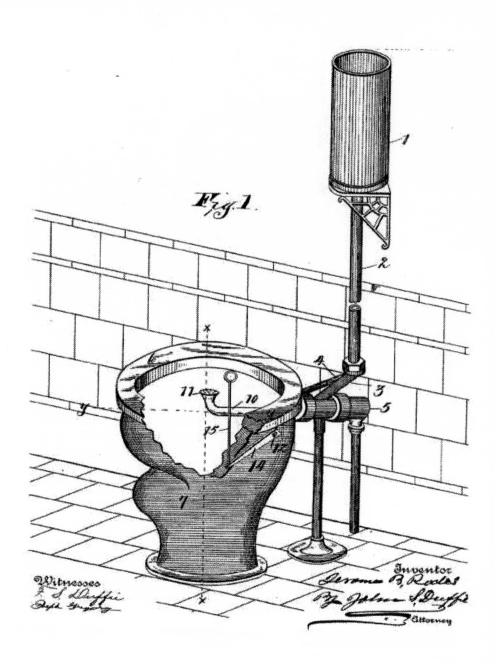

Fig. 1.

The Water Closet

J. B. Rhodes

Invented By
J. B. Rhodes

Patent Date: December 19, 1899
Patent Number: 639,290

There are many names for the water closet, such as: outhouse, commode, toilet. Although a commode, as it is now called, has been around for ages in many different styles, it was not until J. B. Rhodes invented the commode, that people could have privacy and sanitation in their homes.

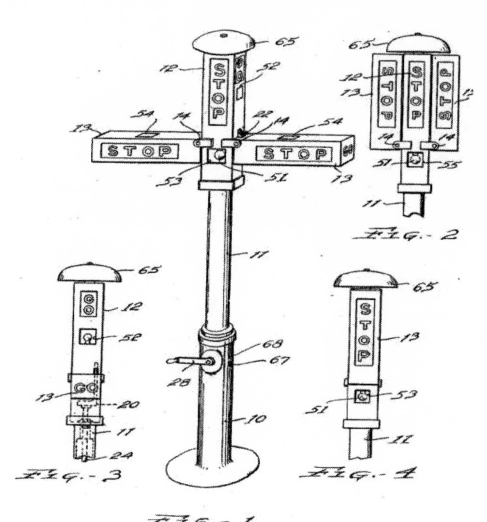

FIG. - 2

FIG. - 3

FIG. - 4

FIG. - 1

INVENTOR
Garrett A. Morgan,
By Bate & Macklin,
ATTORNEYS

Traffic Signal

Garrett A. Morgan

Invented By
Garrett A. Morgan

of
Cleveland, Ohio

Patent Date: November 20, 1923
Patent Number: 1,475,024

The traffic signal, red light, stop light, traffic light is a well-known, valuable and widely used invention. It is a very simple way to maximize safety for individuals who are driving, riding a bike or walking; providing you obey the traffic rules.

The Super-Soaker Water Gun

Lonnie Johnson

Invented By

Lonnie Johnson

of
Atlanta, Georgia

Patent Date: Unknown
Patent Number: Unknown

Millions of kids who own a super soaker can thank Lonnie Johnson for all the hours of fun. He invented this popular toy. More than ten million have been sold in the United States since 1990. Millions more in other countries. This invention allowed Johnson to quit his office job and become a full time inventor.

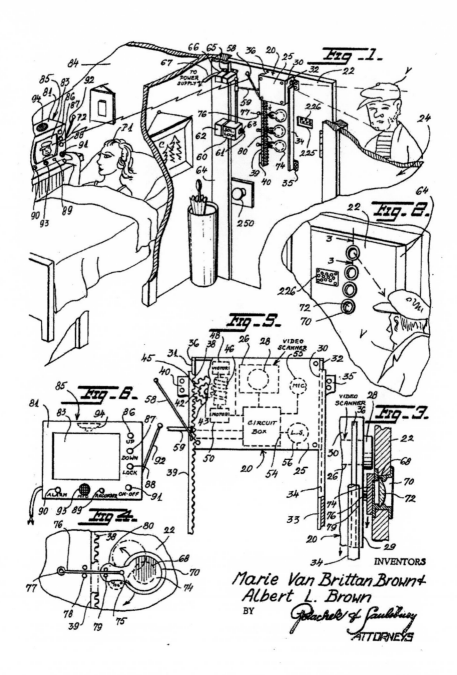

Fig. 1.

Fig. 2.

Fig. 5.

Fig. 6.

Fig. 3.

Fig. 4.

INVENTORS

Marie Van Brittan Brown +
Albert L. Brown
BY

ATTORNEYS

The Home Security System

M. V. B. Brown

Invented By
M. V. B. Brown

of
Jamaica, New York

Patent Date: December 2, 1969
Patent Number: 3,482,037

Many households throughout the world are secured by a home security system other than a lock. Marie's home security system includes a video camera at the entrance door and an audio intercom inside and outside for talking to visitors. Its likeness is used in many homes and building around the world.

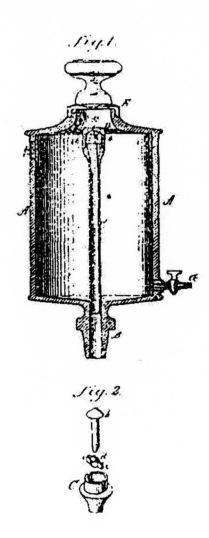

Fig. 1.

Fig. 2.

Witnesses
John A. Ellis
C. Alexander

Inventor
Elijah McCoy
By
J. H. Alexander
Attys

Lubrication Device

Elijah McCoy

Invented By
Elijah McCoy

of
Canada

Patent Date: May 27, 1873
Patent Number: 139,607

If you ever heard the expression, the "Real McCoy" and didn't know how it came to be used or what it was associated with, it was the pioneering work of a black engineer named Elijah McCoy. Elijah invented the automatic lubricator. This is a device that is used to lubricate the axial of trains, trucks and cars and vehicles employing air brakes.   Factories everywhere were investing in McCoy's lubricating cups, and they would always ask the question, is this the "Real McCoy"? They would not accept a substitute. This invention is the forerunner of all lubricating devices that are used in vehicles today.

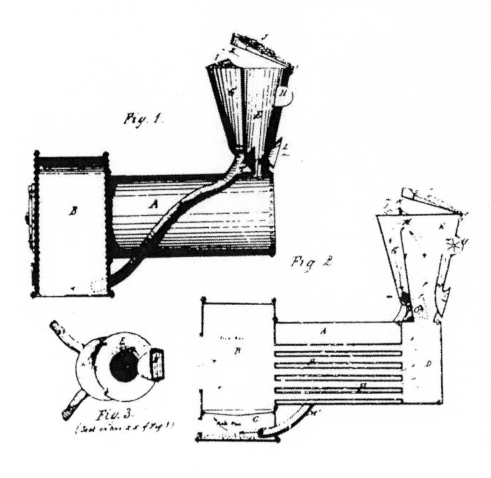

Fig. 1.

Fig 2.

Fig. 3.

The Smoke Stacks for Locomotives

Invented By

Landrow Bell

of
Washington, D.C.

Patent Date: May 23, 1871
Patent Number: 115,153

Sparks and cinders would fly out of stacks, sometimes endangering people and maybe even starting fires along the way from hot cinders or sparks falling on dry grass. Bells' invention of the smoke stack for trains; stopped the flying cinders, and improved the safety of train travel.

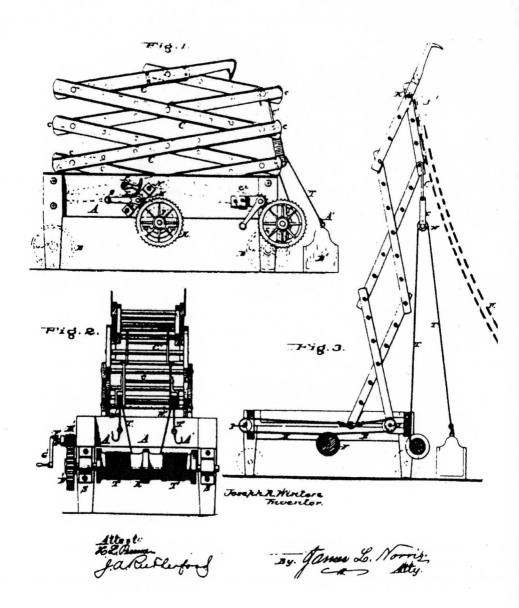

Fig. 1.

Fig. 2.

Fig. 3.

Joseph A. Winters
Inventor.

Attest:
H. L. Benner
J. A. Rutherford

By. James L. Norris.
Atty.

The Fire Escape Ladders

Invented By

Joseph R. Winters

of
Chambersburg, Pennsylvania

Patent Date: May 7, 1878
Patent Number: 203,517

The invention of the fire escape ladder was a very important step for fire fighters. Fire fighters are great people and save many lives and this invention, without question, has helped to make rescue faster and safer.

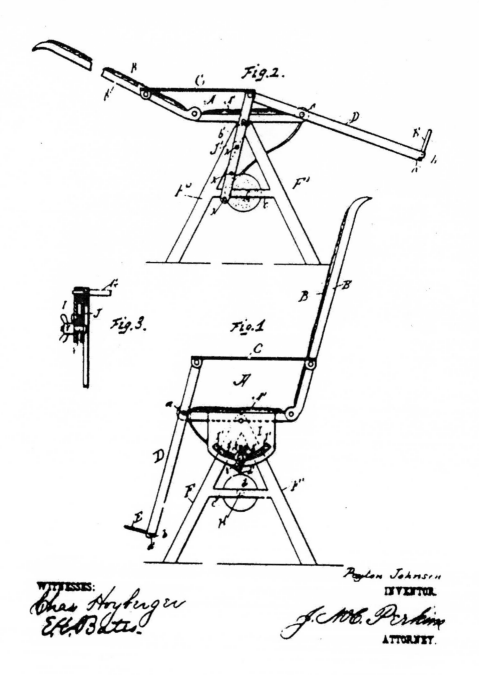

Fig.2.

Fig.3.

Fig.1.

WITNESSES:
Chas Hoyberger
E.H. Bates.

Payton Johnson
INVENTOR

J. M.C. Perkins
ATTORNEY.

The Swinging Chair

Invented By

Payton Johnson

of
Akron, Ohio

Patent Date: November 15, 1881
Patent Number: 249,530

This chair today is known as an easy chair or recliner. It was invented to provide great comfort to the body. Today this invention is Dad's favorite chair for watching TV, or reading the newspaper.

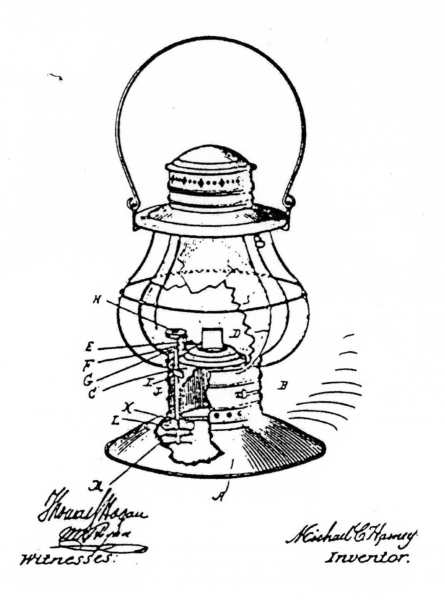

Witnesses:

Michael C. Hpmey
Inventor.

The Lantern or the Lamp

Invented By

M.C. Harney

Patent Date: August 19, 1884
Patent Number: 303,844

Long before the electric light, the lamp was used to light the streets, homes and carriages. It was very dark at night and the lantern could be seen far away, which made it perfect for sending signals to warn train conductors.

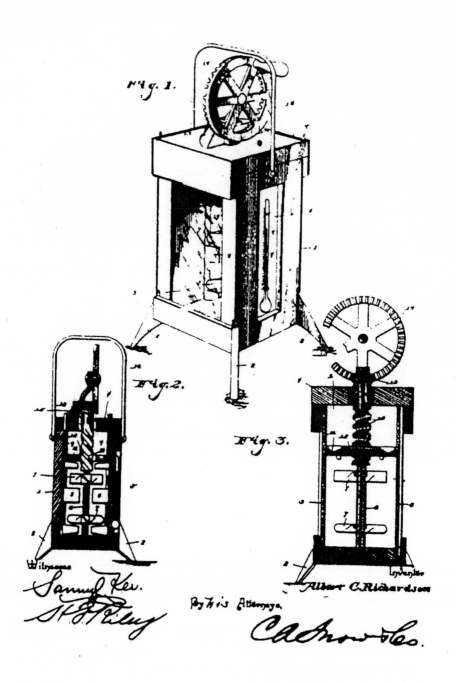

Fig. 1.

Fig. 2.

Fig. 3.

Witnesses

Samuel Ker.

H. T. Riley.

Albert C. Richardson

By his Attorneys

CaSnow & Co.

The Churn

Invented By

Albert C. Richardson

of
South Frankfort, Michigan

Patent Date: February 17, 1891
Patent Number: 446,470

The churn is well-known among dairy farmers. This appliance, shaped like a large jar or barrel with a long wooden stick that looks like a broom stick coming through a hole in the center of the top, is used to make butter from the milk that came directly from the cow.

Albert Richardson improved the churn by putting glass on two sides of the churn so it would be easier to tell when the butter was ready. He also made it easier to remove the butter from the churn, by putting a plate inside the churn for the butter to be placed on.

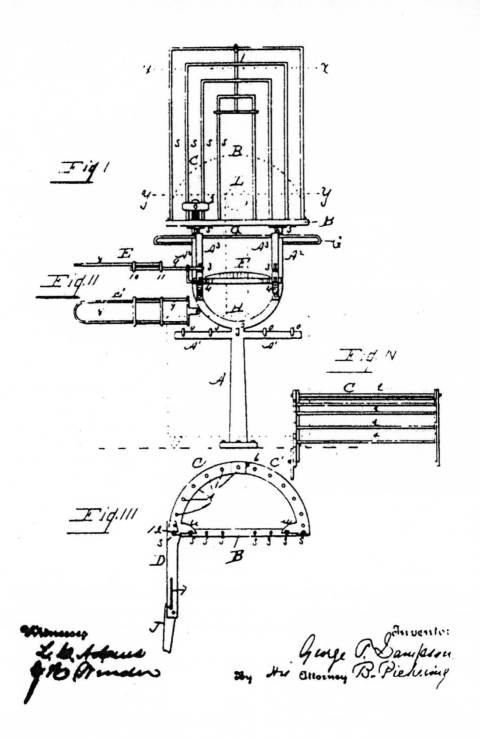

Fig. 1

Fig. II

Fig. IV

Fig. III

Inventor:
George P. Sampson
By His Attorney B. Pickering

The Clothes Drier

Invented By

George T. Sampson

of
Dayton, Ohio

Patent Date: June 7, 1892
Patent Number: 476,416

The clothes drier was a very important invention and has had many improvements. Before the electric drier, clothes were put out on a line to dry in the sunshine where the fresh air could blow on them. Some people even today use this method for drying, but the invention of a portable clothes line that was easy to use and store for drying inside the houses near the stove proved very useful. Now people could dry their clothes, not only during sunny weather, but any time inside the house.

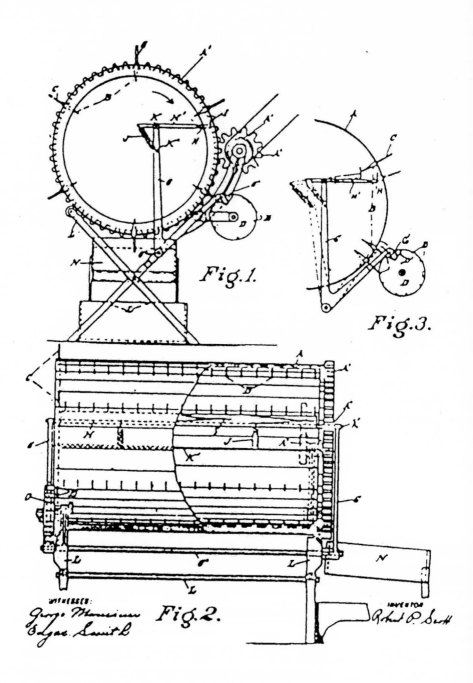

Fig.1.

Fig.3.

Fig.2.

INVENTOR
Robert P. Scott

The Corn Silker

Invented By

R. P. Scott

Patent Date: August 7, 1894
Patent Number: 524,223

If you live in a city, chances are you might not know anything about how corn-on-the-cob is made ready for eating. You must first shuck the corn, which means to remove the outer husks, and the silkier thread fibers called corn silk. These fibers are very difficult and time consuming to remove. Scott's invention made it an easier, faster, and more efficient process.

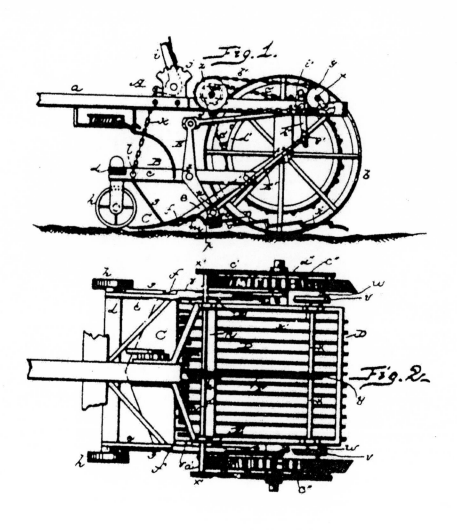

The Potato Digger

Invented By

F. J. Wood

Patent Date: April 23, 1895
Patent Number: 537,953

The potato digger would dig in to the ground to loosen the dirt so it would be easier to remove the potatoes from the ground.

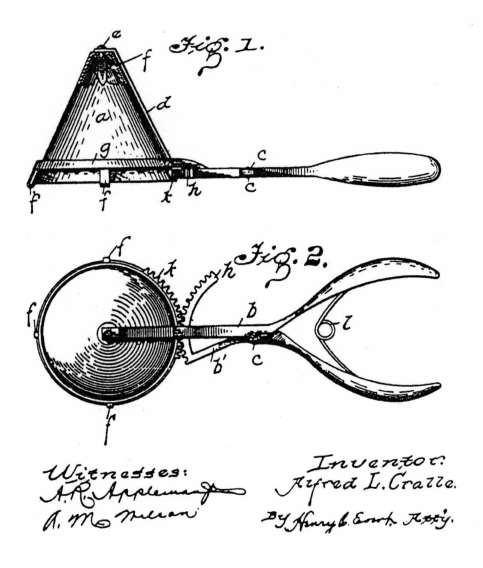

Fig. 1.

Fig. 2.

Witnesses:
A. R. Appleman
A. McMillan

Inventor:
Alfred L. Cralle.
By Henry C. Evans, Atty.

The Ice Cream Mold and Disher / Scoop

Invented By

Alfred L. Cralle

of
Pittsburgh, Pennsylvania

Patent Date: February 2, 1897
Patent Number: 576,395

A "really big thanks" to Alfred Cralle who invented the ice cream disher or scoop as it is called. You can now have a delicious ice cream treat placed neatly on a cone for your enjoyment.

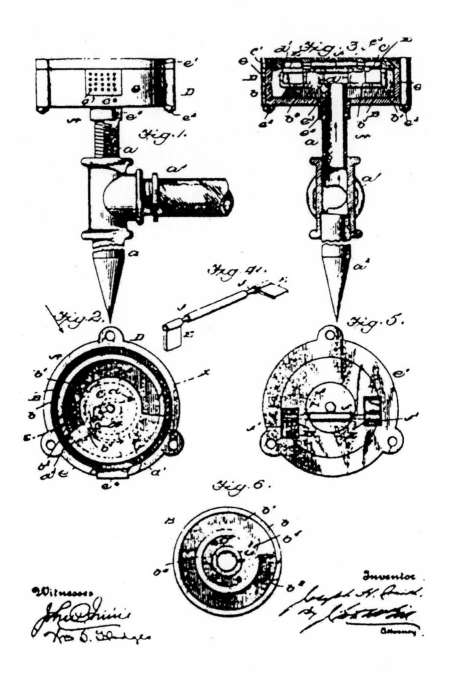

Fig.1.

Fig.3.

Fig.4.

Fig.2.

Fig.5.

Fig.6.

Witnesses

Inventor

Attorney

The Lawn Sprinkler

Invented By

J. H. Smith

Patent Date: May 4, 1897
Patent Number: 581,785

During the summer, the lawn sprinkler is a familiar sight on lawns and parks in many cities and towns throughout the world. The invention of the lawn sprinkler provided a convenient way of watering lawns, gardens and crops.

FIG. 1.

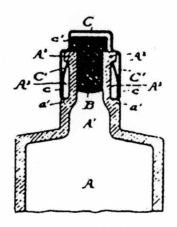

FIG. 2.

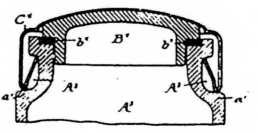

FIG. 3.

FIG. 4.

AMOS E. LONG.
ALBERT A. JONES.
INVENTORS:

WITNESSES:

Frank E. Morley.
E. L. Fullerton.

By Arthur E. Paige
Attorney

The Bottle and Jar Cap

Invented By

De Long
and
A. A. Jones

Patent Date: September 13, 1898
Patent Number: 610,715

Before you drink a bottle of pop or open a jar of peanut butter, you must remove a top. It was this invention by Long and Jones that helped to preserve food long before there were refrigerators. This invention is commonly known to day as the top.

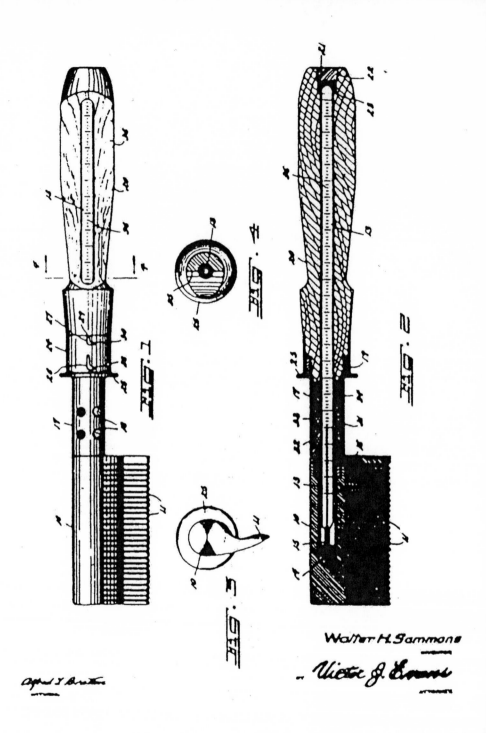

Walter H. Sammons

Victor J. Evans

The Hot Comb

Invented By

W. H. Sammons

Patent Date: December 21, 1920
Patent Number: 1,362,823

The hot comb, or straightening comb as it is sometimes called, is still used

today to press or straighten curly hair of black people.

Black Inventors

INVENTOR	INVENTION	DATE	PATENT
Abrams, W. B.	*Hame attachment*	4/14/1891	450,550
Allen, C. W.	*Self-leveling table*	11/1/1898	613,436
Alien, J. B.	*Clothes line support*	12/10/1895	551,105
Ancker Johnson, B.	*Signal Generator*	11/22/1966	3,287,659
Ashbourne, A. P.	*Process for preparing coconut for*	6/1/1875	163,962
Ashbourne, A. P.	*domestic use*	11/30/1875	170,460
Ashbourne, A. P.	*Biscuit cutter*	7/27/1880	230,518
Ashbourne, A. P.	*Refining coconut oil*	8/21/1877	194,287
Bailes, William	*Process of treating coconut*	8/5/1879	218,154
Bailey, L. C.	*Ladder scaffold-support*	9/25/1883	285,545
Bailey, L. C.	*Combined truss and bandage*	7/18/1899	629,286
Bailiff, C. 0.	*Folding bed*	10/11/1898	612,008
Ballow, W. J.	*Shampoo headrest*	3/29/1898	601,422
Bayliss, R. G. & D. Emrick	*Combined hatrack and tab/e*	2/2/1971	3,565,818
Banres, G. A. E.	*Encapsulation process & its product*	8/19/1889	29,193
Beard, A. J.	*Design for sign*	7/5/1892	478,271
Beard, A. J.	*Rotary engine*	11/23/1897	594,059
Becket, G. E.	*Car-coupler*	10/4/1892	483,525
Bell, L.	*Letter box*	5/23/1871	115,153
Bell, L.	*Locomotive smoke stack*	12/10/1872	133,823
Benjamin, L. W.	*Dough kneader*	5/16/1893	497,747
Benjamin, M. E.	*Broom moisteners and bridles*	7/17/1888	386,286
Binga, M. W.	*Gong and signal chairs for hotels*	7/22/1879	217,843
Blackburn, A. B.	*Street sprinkling apparatus*	1/10/1888	376,362
Blackburn, A. B.	*Railway signal*	4/3/1888	380,420
Blackburn, A. B.	*Spring seat for chairs*	10/23/1888	391,577
Blair, Henry	*Cash carrier*	10/14/1834	NA
Blair, Henry	*Corn planter*	8/31/1836	NA
Blue, L.	*Cotton planter*	5/20/1884	298,937
Bluford, Sr. G. S.	*Hand corn shelling device*	2/13/1951	2,541,025
Booker, L. F.D.	*Artillery Ammunition Training Round Design rubber scraping knife*	3/28/1899	30,404
Boone, Sarah	*Ironing board*	4/26 1892	473,653
Bowmn H. A.	*Making flags*	2/23/1892	469,395
Brook, C. B.	*Punch*	10/31/1893	507,672
Brooks C. B.	*Street-sweepers*	3/17/1896	556,711
Brooks, C. B.	*Street-sweepers*	5/12/1896	560,154
Brooks, Hallstead	*Street-sweepers*	4/21/1896	558,719
Brown, Henry	*Receptacle for storing and preserving papers*	11/2/1886	352,036
Brown, L. F.	*Bridle bit*	10/25/1892	484,994
Brown, 0. E.	*Horseshoe*	8/23/1892	481,271
Brown & Latimer	*Water closets for railway cars*	2/10/1874	147,363
Bundy, R.	*Signal generator*	1/26/1960	2,922,924
Burr, J. A.	*Lawn mower*	5/9/1899	624,749
Burr, W. F.	*Switching device for railways*	10/31/1899	636,197
Burwell, W.	*Boot or shoe*	11/28/1899	638,143
Butler, R. A.	*Train alarm*	6/15/1897	584,540

INVENTOR	INVENTION	DATE	PATENT
Butts, J. W.	*Luggage carrier*	10/10/1899	634,611
Byrd, T. J.	*Improvement in holders for reins for horses*	2/6/1872	123,328
Byrd, T. J.	*Apparatus for detaching horses from carriages*	3/19/1872	124,791
Byrd, T. J.	*Improvement in neck yokes for wagons*	3/19/1872	124,790
Byrd, T. J.	*Improvement in car couplings*	12/1/1874	157,370
Campbell, W. S.	*Self-setting animal trap*	8/30/1881	246,369
Cargill, B. F.	*Invalid cot*	7/25/1899	629,658
Carrington, T. A.	*Range*	7/25/1876	180,323
Carter, W. C.	*Umbrella stand*	8/4/1885	323,397
Carruthers, Geo. R.	*Image converter for Dect Electromagnetic etc.*	11/11/1969	3,478,216
Carter, J. L. & M. Weiner & R. J. Youmans	*Distributed pulse forming network for magnetic modulator*	9/16/1986	4,612,455
Certain, J. M.	*Parcel carrier for bicycles*	12/26/1899	639,708
Cherry, M. A.	*Velocipede*	5/8/1888	382,351
Cherry, M. A.	*Street car fender*	1/1/1895	531,908
Church, T. S.	*Carpet beating machine*	7/29/1884	302,237
Clare, 0. B.	*Trestle*	10/9/1888	390,752
Coates, R.	*Overboot for horses*	4/19/1892	473,295
Cook, G.	*Automatic fishing device*	5/30/1899	625,829
Coolidge, J. S.	*Harness attachment*	11/13/1888	392,908
Cooper, A. R.	*Shoemakers jack*	8/22/1899	631,519
Cooper, J.	*Shutter and fastening*	5/ I/1883	276,563
Cooper, J.	*Elevator device*	4/2/1895	536,605
Cooper, J.	*Elevator device*	9/21/1897	590,257
Cornwell, P. W.	*Draft regulator*	10/2/1888	390,284
Cornwell, P. W.	*Draft regulator*	2/7/1893	491,082
Cralle, A. L.	*Ice-cream mold*	2/2/1897	576,395
Creamer, H.	*Steam feed water trap*	3/17/1895	313,854
Creamer, H.	*Steam trap feeder*	12/11/1888	394,463
Cosgrove, W. F.	*Automatic stop plug for gas oil pipes*	3/17/1885	313,993
Darkins, J. T.	*Ventilation aid (variation)*	2/19/1895	534,322
Davis, I. D.	*Tonic*	11/2/1886	351,829
Davis, W. D.	*Riding saddles*	10/6/1896	568,939
Davis, W. R., Jr.	*Library table*	9/24/1878	208,378
Deitz, W. A.	*Shoe*	4/30/1867	64,205
Dickinson, J. H.	*Pianola*	1899	NA
Dixon Jr. S. & T. R. AuCoin & R. J. Malik	*Monolithic planar doped barrier limiter*	3/31/1987	4,654,609
Dixon Jr. S. & R. J. Malik	*Monolithic planar doped barrier subharmonic mixer*	1/7/1986	4,563,773
Dorsey, 0.	*Door-holding device*	12/10/1878	210,764
Dorticus, C. J.	*Device for applying coloring liquids to sides of soles or heels of shoes*	3/19/1895	535,820
Dorticus, C. J.	*Machine for embossing photo*	4/16/1895	537,442

INVENTOR	INVENTION	DATE	PATENT
Dorticus, C. J.	Photographic print wash	4/23/1875	537,968
Dorticus, C. J.	Hose leak stop	7/18/1899	629,315
Downing, P. B.	Electric switch for railroad	6/17/1890	430,118
Downing, P. B.	Letter box	10/27/1891	462,093
Downing, P. B.	Street letter box	10/27/1891	462,096
Dunnington, J. H.	Horse detachers	3/16/1897	578,979
Edmonds, T. H.	Separating screens	7/20/1897	586,724
Elkins, T.	Dining, ironing table, and quilting frame combined	2/22/1870	700,020
Elkins, T.	Chamber commode	1/9/1872	122,518
Elkins, T.	Refrigerating apparatus	11/4/1879	221,222
Evans, J. H.	Convertible settees	10/5/1897	591,095
Faulkner, H.	Ventilated shoe	4/29/1890	426,495
Ferrell, F. J.	Steam trap	2/11/1890	420,993
Ferrell, F. J.	Apparatus for melting snow	5/27/1890	428,670
Fisher, D.	Joiners' clamp	4/20/1875	162,281
Fisher, D. C.	Furniture castor	3/14/1876	174,794
Flemming, F., Jr.	Guitar (variation)	3/3/1886	338.727
Forten, J.	Sail control (described in Mass. Newspaper)	1850	NA
Goode, Sarah E.	Folding cabinet bed	7/14/1885	322,177
Gourdine, M. C.	Electrogas dynamic mtd. & apparatus	6/10/1969	3,449,667
Grant, G. F.	Golf tee	12/12/1899	638,920
Grant, W.	Curtain rod support	8/4/1896	565,075
Gray, R. H.	Bailing press	8/28/1894	525,203
Gray, R. H.	Cistern cleaners	4/9/1895	537,151
Gregory, J.	Motor	4/26/1887	361,937
Grenon, H.	Razor stropping device	2/18/1896	554,867
Griffin, F. W.	Pool table attachment	6/13/1899	626,902
Gunn, S. W.	Boot or shoe (variation)	1/16/1900	641,642
Haines, J. H.	Portable basin	9/28/1897	590,833
Hale, Wm.	An improvement in airplanes	4/7/1925	1,563,278
Hall, Lloyd A.	Manuf. Stable dry papain composition	3/15/1949	2,464,200
Hall, Lloyd A.	Asphalt emulsion & manuf. Thereof	10/18/1932	1,882,834
Hall, Lloyd A.	Sterilizing foodstuff	2/8/1938	2,107,697
Hall, Lloyd A.	Puncture sealing composition & manuf. thereof	9/5/1944	2,357,650
Hammonds, J. F.	Apparatus for holding yarn skeins	12/15/1896	572,985
Harding, F. H.	Extension banquet table	11/22/1898	614,468
Harper, Solomon	Electric hair treatment	8/5/1930	1,772,002
Harper, Solomon	Thermostatic Control Hair Curlers	8/8/1953	2,648,757
Harper, S.	Thermostatic Controlled Fur etc.	8/11/1953	2,711,095
Hawkins, J.	Gridiron	3/26/1845	3,973
Hawkins, R.	Harness attachment	10/4/1887	370,943
Headen, M.	Foot power hammer	10/5/1886	350,363
Hearness, R.	Detachable car fender	7/4/1899	628. 003
Hilyer, A. F.	Water evaporator attachment for hot air registers	8/26/1890	435,095
Hilyer, A. F.	Registers	10/14/1890	438,159
Holmes, E. H.	Gage	11/12/1895	549,513

INVENTOR	INVENTION	DATE	PATENT
Hunter, J. H.	Portable weighing scales	11/3/1896	570,553
Hyde, R. N.	Composition for cleaning and preserving carpets	11/6/1888	392, 205
Jackson, B. F.	Heating apparatus	3/1/1898	599,985
Jackson, B. F.	Matrix drying apparatus	5/10/1898	603,879
Jackson, B. F.	Gas burner	4/4/1899	622,482
Jackson, H. A.	Kitchen table (variation)	10/5/1898	569,135
Jackson, W. H.	Railway switch	3/9/1897	578,641
Jackson, W. H.	Railway switch	3/16/1897	593,665
Jackson, W. H.	Automatic locking switch	8/23/1898	609,436
Johnson, D.	Rotary dining table	1/15/1888	396,089
Johnson, D.	Lawn mower attachment	9/10/1889	410,836
Johnson, D.	Grass receivers for lawn mowers	6/10/1890	429,629
Johnson, I.R.	Bicycle frame	10/10/1899	634,823
Johnson, P.	Swinging chairs	11/15/1881	249,530
Johnson, P.	Eye protector	11/2/1880	234,039
Johnson, W.	Egg beater	2/5/1884	292,821
Johnson, W.	Velocipede	6/20/1899	627,335
Johnson, W.A.	Paint vehicle	12/4/1888	393,763
Johnson, W.H.	Overcoming dead centers	2/4/1896	554,223
Johnson, W.H.	Overcoming dead centers	10/11/1898	612,345
Jones, F. M.	Ticket dispensing machine	6/27/1939	2,163,754
Jones, F. M.	Air conditioning unit	7/12/1949	2,475,841
Jones, F. M.	Two-cycle gasoline engine	11/28/1950	2,523,273
Jones, F. M.	Starter generator	7/12/1949	2,475,842
Jones, F. M.	Thermostat and temperature control system	2/23/1960	2,926,005
Jones & Long	Caps for bottles	9/13/1898	610,715
Joyce, J.A.	Ore bucket	4/26/1898	603,143
Juliain, Hubert	Airplane safety device	5/24/1921	1,379,264
Julian, Percy L.	Preparation of cortisone	8/10/1954	2,752,339
Julian, P.C. et al.	Recovery of sterols	10/22/1940	2,718,971
Latimer, L. H.	Lamp fixture	8/10/1910	968,787
Latimer, L. H.	Manufacturing carbons	6/17/1882	252,386
Latimer, L. H.	Apparatus for cooling and disinfecting	1/12/1886	334,078
Latimer, L. H.	Locking rack for hats, coats, and umbrellas	3/24/1896	557,076
Latimer & Nichols	Electric lamp	9/13/1881	247,097
Latimer & Tregoning	Globe support for electric lamps	3/21/1882 9/17/1878	255,212 208,208
Lavalette, W.	Printing press	2/12/1867	61,941
Lee, H.	Animal trap	8/7/1894	524,042
Lee, J.	Kneading machine	6/4/1895	540,553
Lee, J.	Bread crumbling machine	9/21/1897	590,325
Leslie, F. W.	Envelope seal	9/27/1892	483,359
Lewis, A. L.	Window cleaner	5/3/1887	362,096
Lewis, E. R.	Spring gun	9/8/1891	459,365
Linden, H.	Piano truck	3/7/1882	254,666
Little, E.	Bridle-bit	12/12/1892	510,432
Loudin, F. J.	Sash fastener	1/9/1894	512,308

INVENTOR	INVENTION	DATE	PATENT
Loudin, F. J.	*Key fastener*	7/9/1895	542,419
Love, J. L.	*Plasterers' hawk*	11/23/1897	594,114
Love, J. L.	*Pencil sharpener*	5/26/1872	125,063
Marshall, T. J.	*Fire extinguisher (variation)*		
Marshall, W.	*Grain binder*	5/11/1886	341,599
Martin, W. A.	*Lock*	7/23/1889	407,738
Martin, W. A.	*Lock*	12/30/1890	443,945
Matzeliger, J. E.	*Mechanism for distributing tacks*	11/26/1899	415,726
Matzeliger, J. E.	*Nailing machine*	2/25/1896	421,954
Matzeliger, J. E.	*Tack separating mechanism*	Mar/25/1890	423,937
Matzeliger, J. E.	*Lasting machine*	3/20/1883	274,207
McCoy, E.	*Lubricator for steam engines*	7/2/1872	129,843
McCoy, E.	*Lubricator for steam engines*	8/6/1872	130,305
McCoy, E.	*Steam lubricator*	1/20/1874	146,697
McCoy, E.	*Ironing table*	5/12/1874	150,876
McCoy, E.	*Steam cylinder lubricator*	2/1/1876	173,032
McCoy, E.	*Steam cylinder lubricator*	7/4/1876	179,585
McCoy, E.	*Lawn sprinkler design*	9/26/1899	631,549
McCoy, E.	*Steam dome*	6/16/1885	320,354
McCoy, E.	*Lubricator attachment*	4/19/1887	361,435
McCoy, E.	*Lubricator for safety valves*	5/24/1887	363,529
McCoy, E.	*Drip cup*	9/29/1891	460,215
McCoy & Hodges	*Lubricator*	12/24/1889	418,139
McCree, D.	*Portable fire escape*	11/11/1890	440,322
Mendenhall, A.	*Holder for driving reins*	11/28/1899	637,811
Miles, A.	*Elevator*	10/11/1887	371,207
Mitchell, C. L.	*Phoneterism*	1/1/1884	291,071
Mitchell, J. M.	*Check row corn planter*	1/16/1900	641,462
Moody, W. U.	*Game board design*	5/11/1897	27,046
Morehead, K.	*Reel carrier*	10/6/1896	568,916
Murray, G. W.	*Combined furrow opener and stalk-knocker*	4/10/1894	517,960
Murray, G. W.	*Cultivator and marker*	4/10/1894	517,961
Murray, G. W.	*Planter*	6/5/1894	520,887
Murray, G. W.	*Cotton chopper*	6/5/1894	520,888
Murray, G. W.	*Fertilizer distributor*	6/5/1894	520,889
Murray, G. W.	*Planter*	6/5/1894	520,891
Murray, G. W.	*Planter and fertilizer distributor reaper*	6/5/1894	520,892
Murray, W.	*Attachment for bicycles*	1/27/1891	445,452
Nance, L.	*Game apparatus*	12/1/1891	464,035
Nash, H. H.	*Life-preserving stool*	10/5/1875	168,519
Newson, S.	*Oil heater or cooker*	5/22/1894	520,188
Nichols & Latimer	*Electric lamp (variation)*	9/13/1881	247,097
Nickerson, W. J.	*Mandolin and guitar attachment for pianos*	6/27/1899	627,739
O'Conner & Turner		8/25/1896	566,612
O'Conner & Turner	*Alarm for boilers*	8/25/1896	566,613
O'Conner & Turner	*Steam gage*	2/8/1898	598,572
	Alarm for coasts containing vessels	11/15/1898	614,273
Outlaw, J. W.	*Horseshoes*	2/2/1892	468,038
Perryman, F. R.	*Caterers' tray table*	11/8/1966	3,284,239

INVENTOR	INVENTION	DATE	PATENT
Perry, John Jr. & Hunger H. F.	Biochem fuel cell	4/30/1889	402,189
Peterson, H.	Attachment for lawn mowers	3/23/1897	579,242
Helps, W. H.	Apparatus for washing vehicles	2/20/1900	643,975
Pickering, J. F.	Air ship		
Pickett, H.	Scaffold	6/30/1874	152,511
Pinn, T. B.	File holder	8/17/1880	231,355
Polk, A. J.	Bicycle support	4/14/1896	558,103
Prather, Al. G. B.	Man powered glider aircraft	2/6/1973	3,715,Oll
Pugsley, A.	Blind stop	7/29/1890	433,306
Purdy, W.	Device for sharpening edged tools	10/27/1896	570,337
Purdy, W.	Device for sharpening edged tools	8/16/1898	609,367
Purdy, W.	Device for sharpening edged tools	8/1/18996	30,106
Purdy & Peters	Design for spoons	4/23/1895	24,228
Purdy & Sadgwar	Folding chair	6/11/1889	405,117
Purvis, W. B.	Bag fastener	4/25/1882	256,856
Purvis, W. B.	Hand stamp	2/27/1883	273,149
Purvis, W. B.	Fountain pen	1/7/1890	419,065
Purvis, W. B.	Electric railway (variation)	5/1/1894	519,291
Purvis, W. B.	Magnetic car balancing device	5/21/1895	539,542
Purvis, W. B.	Electric railway switch	8/17/1897	588,176
Queen. W.	Guard for companion ways and hatches	8/18/1891	458,131
Ray. E. P.	Chair supporting device	2/21/1899	620,078
Ray, L. P.	Dust pan	8/3/1897	587,607
Reed. J. W.	Dough kneader and roller	9/23/1884	305,474
Reynolds, H. H.	Window ventilator for railroad cars	4/3/1883	275,271
Reynolds, H. H.	Safety gate for bridges	10/7/1890	437,937
Reynolds, R. R.	Nonrefillable bottle	5/2/1899	624,092
Rhodes, J. B.	Water closets	12/19/1899	639,290
Richardson, A. C.	Hame fastener	3/14/1882	255,022
Richardson, A. C.	Chum	2/17/1891	466,470
Richardson, A. C.	Casket-lowering device	11/13/1894	529,311
Richardson, A. C.	Insect destroyer	2/28/1899	620,363
Richardson, A. C.	Bottle	12/12/1899	638,811
Richardson, W. H.	Cotton chopper	6/1/1886	343,140
Richardson, W. H.	Child's carriage	6/18/1889	405,599
Richardson, W. H.	Child's carriage	6/18/1889	405,600
Richey, C. V.	Car coupling	6/15/1897	584,650
Richey, C. V.	Railroad switch	8/3/1897	587,657
Richey, C. V.	Railroad switch	10/26/1897	592,448
Richey, C. V.	Fire escape bracket	12/28/1897	596,427
Richey, C. V.	Combined hammock and stretcher	12/13/1898	615,907
Rickman, A. L.	Overshoe	2/8/1898	598,816
Ricks, J.	Horseshoe	3/30/1886	338,781
Ricks, J.	Overshoes for horses	6/6/1899	626,245
Rillieux, N.	Sugar refiner (evaporating pan)	12/10/1846	4,879
Robinson, E. R.	Electric railway trolley	9/19/1893	505,370
Robinson, E. R.	Casting composite	11/23/1897	594,386
Robinson, J. H.	Lifesaving guards for locomotives	3/14/1899	621,143
Robinson, J. H.	Lifesaving guards for street cars	4/25/1899	623,929

INVENTOR	INVENTION	DATE	PATENT
Robinson, J.	*Dinner pail*	2/1/1887	356,852
Romain, A.	*Passenger register*	4/23/1889	402,035
Ross, A. L.	*Runner for stops*	8/4/1896	565,301
Ross, A. L.	*Bag closure*	6/7/1898	605,343
Ross, A. L.	*Trousers support*	11/28/1899	638,068
Ross, J.	*Bailing press*	9/5/1899	632,539
Roster, D. N.	*Feather curler*	3/10/1896	556,166
Ruffin, S.	*Vessels for liquids and manner of sealing*	11/20/1899	737. 603
Russell, L. A.	*Guard attachment for beds*	8/13/1895	544,381
Sampson, G. T.	*Sled propeller*	2/17/1885	312,388
Sampson, G. T.	*Clothes drier*	6/7/1892	476,416
Scottron, S. R.	*Adjustable window cornice*	2/17/1880	224,732
Scottron, S. R.	*Cornice*	1/16/1883	270,851
Scottron, S. R.	*Pole tip*	9/21/1886	349,525
Scottron, S. R.	*Curtain rod*	8/30/1892	481,720
Scottron, S. R.	*Supporting bracket*	9/21/1893	505,008
Shanks, S. C.	*Sleeping car berth register*	7/21/1897	587,165
Shewcraft, Frank	*Letter box*	NA	NA
Shorter, D. W.	*Feed rack*	5/17/1887	363,089
Smith, B. & L. E. Branovich, & G. L. Freeman	*Mtd. Or preparing nonlaminating anisotropic boron Nitride*	10/1/1985	4,544,535
Smith, J. W.	*Improvement in games*	4/17/1900	647,887
Smith, J. W.	*Lawn sprinkler*	5/4/1897	581,785
Smith, J. W.	*Lawn sprinkler*	3/22/1898	601,065
Smith, P. D.	*Potato digger*	1/21/1891	445,206
Smith, P. D.	*Grain binder*	2/23/1892	469,279
Snow & Johns	*Liniment*	10/7/1890	437,728
Spears, H.	*Portable shield for infantry*	12/27/1870	110,599
Spikes, R. B.	*Combination milk bottle opener and bottle cover*	6/29/1926	1,590,557
Spikes, R. B.	*Method and apparatus for obtaining average samples and temperature of tank liquids*	10/27/1931	1,828,753
Spikes, R. B.	*Automatic gear shift*	12/6/1932	1,889,814
Spikes, R. B.	*Transmission and shifting thereof*	11/28/1933	1,936,996
Spikes, R. B.	*Self-locking rack for billiard cues*	ca. 1910	NA
Spikes, R. B.	*Automatic shoeshine chair*	ca. 1939	NA
Spikes, R. B.	*Multiple barrel machine gun*	ca. 1940	NA
Standard, J.	*Oil stove*	10/29/1889	413,689
Standard, J.	*Refrigerator*	7/14/1891	455,891
Stewart, E. W.	*Punching machine*	5/3/1887	362,190
Stewart, E. W.	*Machine for forming vehicle seat bars*	3/22/1887	373,698
Stewart, T. W.	*Mop*	6/13/1893	499,402
Stewart, T. W.	*Station indicator*	6/20/1893	499,895
Stewart & Johnson	*Metal bending machine*	12/27/1887	375,512
Sutton, J. A.	*Cotton cultivator*	4/7/1878	149,543
Sweeting, J. A.	*Device for rolling cigarettes*	11/30/1897	594,501
Sweeting, J. A.	*Combined knife and scoop*	6/7/1898	605,209

INVENTOR	INVENTION	DATE	PATENT
Taylor, B. H.	*Rotary engine*	4/23/1878	202,888
Taylor, B. H.	*Side valve*	7/6/1897	585,798
Temple, L.	*Toggle harpoon*	1848	
Thomas, S. E.	*Waste trap*	10/16/1883	286,746
Thomas, S. E.	*Waste trap for basins, closets, etc.*	10/4/1887	371,107
Thomas, S. E.	*Casting*	7/31/1888	386,941
Thomas, S. E.	*Pipe connection*	10/9/1888	390,821
Toliver, George	*Propeller for vessels*	4/28/1891	451,086
Tregoning & Latimer	*Globe supporter for electric lamps*	3/21/1882	255,212
Walker, Peter	*Machine for cleaning seed cotton*	2/16/1897	577,153
Walker, Peter	*Bait holder*	3/8/1898	600,241
Waller, J. N.	*Shoemaker's cabinet or bench*	2/3/1880	244,253
Washington, Wade	*Corn husking machine*	8/14/1883	283,173
Watkins, Isaac	*Scrubbing frame*	10/7/1890	437,849
Watts, J. R.	*Bracket for mines' lamp*	3/7/1893	493,137
West, E. H.	*Weather shield*	9/5/1899	632,385
West, J. W.	*Wagon*	10/18/1870	108,419
White, D. L.	*Extension steps for cars*	1/12/1897	574,969
White, J. T.	*Lemon Squeezer*	12/8/1896	572,849
Williams, Carter	*Canopy frame*	2/2/1892	468,280
Williams, J. P.	*Pillow sham holder*	10/10/1899	634,784
Winn, Frank	*Direct acting steam engine*	12/4/1888	394,047
Winters, J. R.	*Fire escape ladder*	5/7/1878	203,517
Winters, J. R.	*Fire escape ladder*	4/8/1879	214,224
Woods, G. T.	*Steam boiler furnace*	6/3/1884	299,894
Woods, G. T.	*Telephone transmitter (variation)*	12/2/1884	308,176
Woods, G. T.	*Apparatus for transmission of messages by electricity*	4/7/1885	315,368
Woods, G. T.	*Relay instrument*	6/7/1887	364,619
Woods, G. T.	*Polarized relay*	7/5/1887	366,192
Woods, G. T.	*Electromechanical brake*	8/16/1887	368,265
Woods, G. T.	*Telephone system and apparatus*	10/11/1887	371,241
Woods, G. T.	*Electromagnetic brake apparatus*	10/18/1887	371,655
Woods, G. T.	*Railway telegraphy*	11/15/1887	373,383
Woods, G. T.	*Induction telegraph system*	11/29/1887	373,915
Woods, G. T.	*Overhead conducting system for electric railway*	5/29/1888	383,844
Woods, G. T.	*Electromotive railway system*	6/26/1888	385,034
Woods, G. T.	*Tunnel construction for electric railway*	7/17/1888	388,803
Woods, G. T.	*Galvanic battery*	8/14/1888	387,839
Woods, G. T.	*Railway telegraphy*	8/28/1888	388,803
Woods, G. T.	*Automatic safety cut-out for electric circuits*	1/1/1889	395,533
Woods, G. T.	*Automatic safety cut-out for electric circuits*	10/14/1889	438,590
Woods, G. T.	*Electric railway system*	11/10/1891	463,020
Woods, G. T.	*Electric railway supply system*	10/31/1893	507,606
Woods, G. T.	*Electric railway conduit*	11/21/1893	509,065
Woods, G. T.	*System of electrical distribution*	10/13/1896	569,443

INVENTOR	INVENTION	DATE	PATENT
Woods, G. T.	*Amusement apparatus*	12/19/1899	639,692
Wormley, James	*Lifesaving apparatus*	5/24/1881	242,091

SKETCHES

OF

BLACK INVENTORS

FROM

THE SIDNEY WALLACE BLACK INVENTORS COLLECTION

FRAME
AND
DISPLAY
YOUR FAVORITE
INVENTOR

You may secure information on how to order a framed
drawing of each inventor by writing to the following address:
S&M Wallace Enterprises
328 Stoney Creek Rd. NW
Cedar Rapids, Iowa 52405

Norman Rillieux
Sugar Refinement

A.P. Ashborne

Biscuit Cutter

DAVID JOHNSON

W.A. Lavalette
Printing Press

DAVID
JOHNSON

Lewis H. Latimer
Incandescent Light-Bulb

DAVID JOHNSON

Jan E. Matzeliger
Shoe Lasting Machine

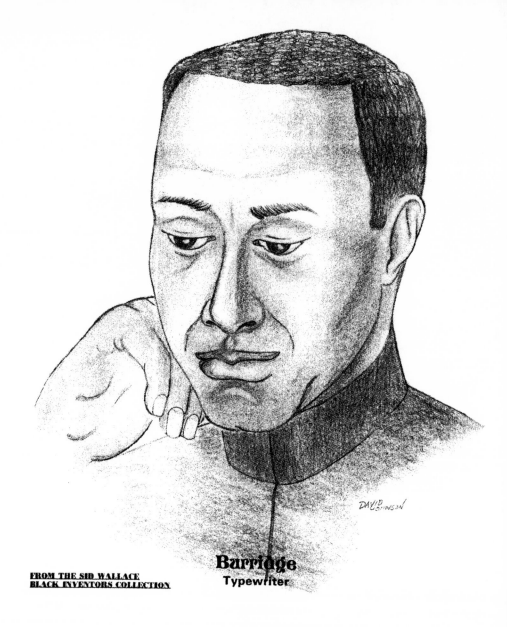

Burridge
Typewriter

W. Johnson
Egg Beater

William D. Davis
Horse Riding Saddle

Robert Flemming Jr.
Guitar

DAVID JOHNSON

L.P. Ray
Dust Pan

W.H. Richardson
Baby Buggy

DAVID JOHNSON

Granville T. Woods
Boiler Furnace

W.B. Purvis
Fountain Pen

John Stanard   David Johnson
Refrigerator

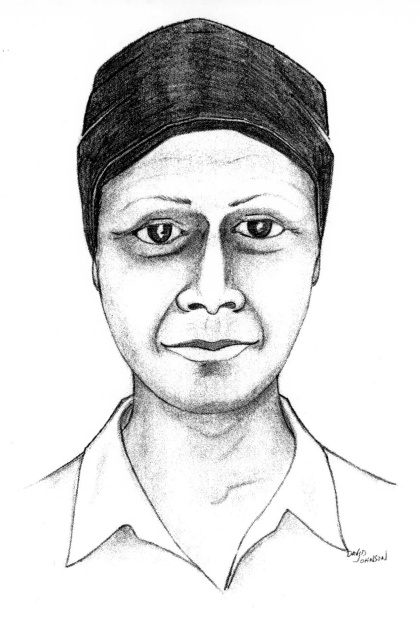

Sarah Boone

Ironing Board

Oscar B. Brown

Horse Shoe

T.W. Stewart
Mop

Lydia Newman
Hair Brush

DAVID
JOHNSON

XXII

George F. Grant
Golf Tee

Issac R. Johnson
Bicycle Frame

DAVID
JOHNSON

Garrett Morgan
Electric Traffic Signal

Marie V. Brittan Brown

Home Security System

Alexander Miles
Elevator

Solomon Harper
Electric Hair Comb

David Johnson

G.E. Becket
Mail Box

E. Little
Bridle-Bit

DAVID JOHNSON

T. Elkins
Toilet (Commode)

Madame C. J. Walker

Hair Care Product